This book belongs to:
....

Dear Tash,
May you have many great adventures!
Best wishes,
Chloe

"The mountains are calling and I must go."
— John Muir

"The mountains are calling and I must go."
— John Muir

In Wasdale on a Cumbrian farm

is where we begin this Lakeland yarn.

On a farm called Middle Row

lived a lad named Joss who you might know.

Joss grafted hard

in the sunshine and sleet.

He fed
the chickens

and sheared
the sheep.

At four years old, up Haycock
he sat upon a craggy rock.

He watched the sheep coming up the pass,
trotting through the gate, a winding mass.

Accompanied by his loyal sheep dog Bell,
Joss looked across the sprawling fell.

That was where it all began,
where he jumped up and where he RAN.

He ran up the fell
through peaty bogs,
he ran through woods
and over logs.

He ran until he
conquered the top,
reaching out,
he touched a rock.

He ran until he reached a stack, he ran along the lush green track.

He ran through rain and wind and hail, he felt like he could never fail.

Joss ran below an endless sky,

he ran as if a man could fly.

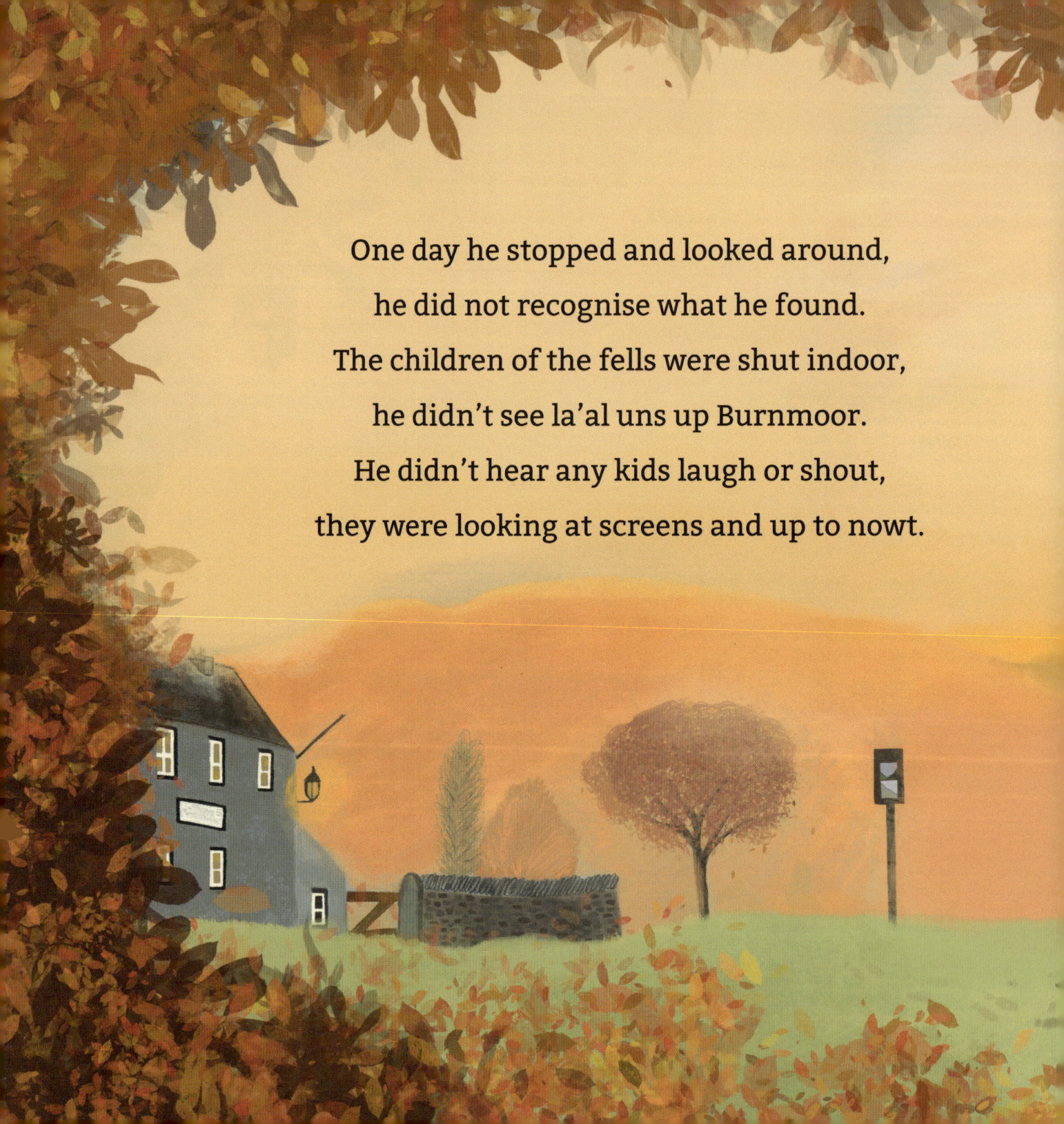

One day he stopped and looked around,
he did not recognise what he found.
The children of the fells were shut indoor,
he didn't see la'al uns up Burnmoor.
He didn't hear any kids laugh or shout,
they were looking at screens and up to nowt.

Joss had an idea, a brainwave,
a little thought which
caught and stayed.

"I will hold a race," he thought.

"To teach them things that can't be taught.

I will get them out to play a game."

So, he did and yes, they came!

He pointed up yonder and over Lingmell,

"That there, kids, is mighty Kirkfell.

I wonder if any of you can reach the top.

I wonder how many of you will stop."

They all ran down, they all ran up, the children ran right through the muck.

Some of the children started to sing
as they ran through the winter sting.

Some lost their wellies, some lost their socks,
yet no one stopped till they reached the top.

They ran through rain, they ran through hail,
Joss made them feel they couldn't fail.

They ran below an endless sky,
they felt as if they could fly.

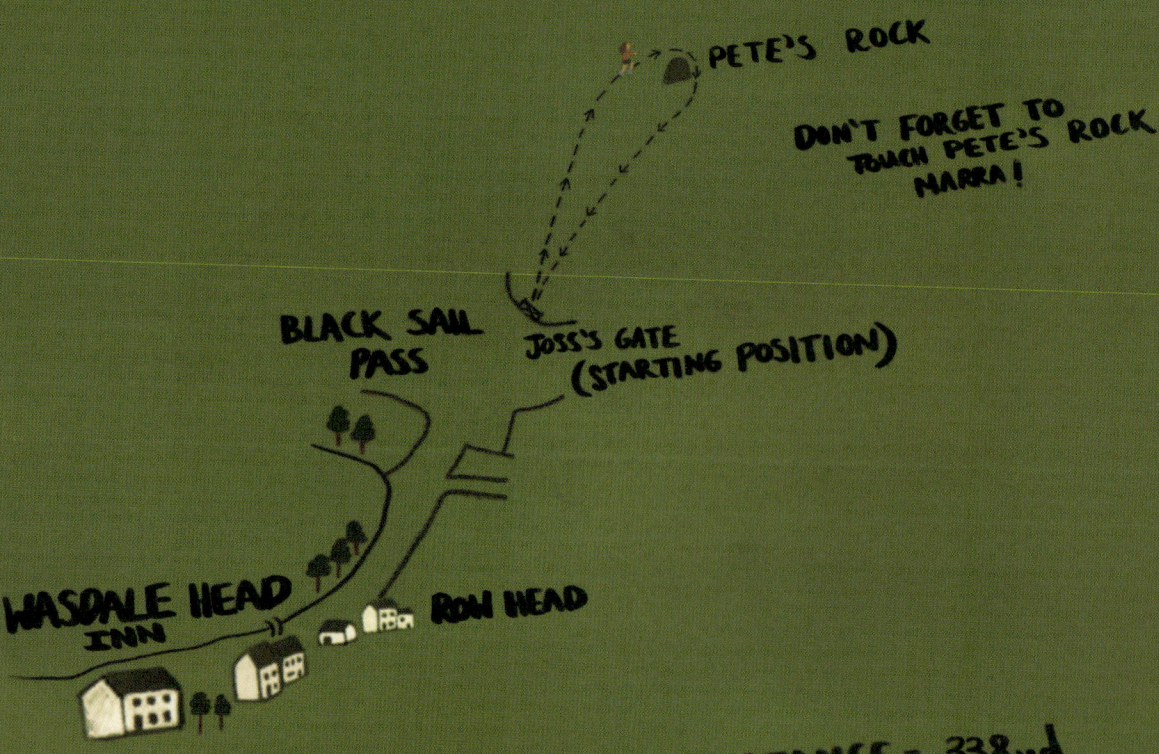

A note to the reader from Joss Naylor MBE

"I was born on the 10th of February 1936 in Middle Row Farm, Wasdale Head. I worked on the family farm when I was a la'al lad, my first job was feeding the chickens. I've been a fell runner and I've run many a race, earning the title King of the Fells. Now I would like to set you a running challenge."

Follow the map to run Joss' Junior Kirk Fell Challenge. If you wish please use the QR code to tell us your completion time, which we will record and share annually.
Good luck marra.

Joss' tips for runners

The hardest bit of a run is the first few steps

Dig in if it gets hard. The good feelings will come soon

If you start the run always finish the run

As you run take some time to look around where you are. The world around you is an amazing place

Don't forget to tie your laces

'For Aurora and her wild spirit'
Mum

A special thank you to Peter Todhunter and Joss Naylor MBE, without you this book would not be possible.

Text and illustrations copyright © Chloë Wilson 2023.

The right of Chloë Wilson to be identified as the author and illustrator of this work has been asserted by them in accordance with the Copyright, Designs and Patents Act 1988.

Thanks to editor - Mollie Bryde-Evens
Graphic Designer - Megan Winter-Barker
First published by Wrybill Books in 2023

ISBN 978-1-7393621-0-2

Fifty pence from this copy goes to the Brathay Trust on behalf of Joss Naylor MBE, we proudly support this charity.

CONNECT WITH US:
@chlointhelakes | @wrybillbooks